72611
The Colorado River

W9-CNW-142

Points: 1.0

The **Colorado** River

by Daniel Gilpin

Gareth Stevens Publishing
A WORLD ALMANAC EDUCATION GROUP COMPANY

Please visit our web site at: www.garethstevens.com
For a free color catalog describing Gareth Stevens Publishing's list of high-quality books and multimedia programs, call 1-800-542-2595 (USA) or 1-800-387-3178 (Canada). Gareth Stevens Publishing's fax: (414) 332-3567.

Library of Congress Cataloging-in-Publication Data

Gilpin, Daniel.
    The Colorado River / by Daniel Gilpin.
       p. cm. — (Rivers of North America)
    Includes bibliographical references and index.
    Contents: The lifeline of the Southwest—From source to mouth—The life of the river—
A river in the desert—Taming the wild river—Places to visit—How rivers form.
    ISBN 0-8368-3753-3 (lib. bdg.)
    1. Colorado River (Colo.-Mexico)—Juvenile literature. [1. Colorado River (Colo.-Mexico).]
I. Title. II. Series.
F788.G5   2003
979.1'3—dc21   2003042798

This North American edition first published in 2004 by
Gareth Stevens Publishing
A World Almanac Education Group Company
330 West Olive Street, Suite 100
Milwaukee, Wisconsin 53212 USA

Original copyright © 2004 The Brown Reference Group plc. This U.S. edition copyright © 2004 by Gareth Stevens, Inc.

Author: Daniel Gilpin
Editor: Tom Jackson
Consultant: Judy Wheatley Maben, Education Director, Water Education Foundation
Designer: Steve Wilson
Cartographer: Mark Walker
Picture Researcher: Clare Newman
Indexer: Kay Ollerenshaw
Managing Editor: Bridget Giles
Art Director: Dave Goodman

Gareth Stevens Editor: Betsy Rasmussen
Gareth Stevens Designer: Melissa Valuch

Picture Credits: Cover: The Grand Canyon, Arizona. (Skyscan: Jim Wark)
Contents: Hoover Dam, Arizona.

Key: l–left, r–right, t–top, b–bottom.
Ardea: Ian Beames 21; Francois Gohier 5b; Arizona Office of Tourism: 26b, 29b; Corbis: E. O. Beaman 16; Tom Bean 12,14; Richard Cummins 18/19; Ric Ergenbright 7; Annie Griffiths Belt 9t; Robert Holmes 4/5; David Muench 28; NASA 22; Charles O'Rear 20; Ted Spiegel 26t; Robert B. Stanton 18; Ron Watts 17; Library of Congress: 23; National Archives: 15t, 15b; PhotoDisc: Larry Brownstein 29t; Robert Glusic 24t; Scencis of America/Photolink 27; Jeremy Woodhouse 8/9, 24/25; Still Pictures: Brookshier-UNEP 8t; William Campbell 4b; Daniel Heuclin 13b; Klein/Hubert 11; Sylvia Cordaiy Picture Library: 10; Tom Brennan: 13t

Printed in the United States of America

1 2 3 4 5 6 7 8 9 07 06 05 04 03

Table of Contents

The Lifeline of the Southwest

The Colorado River flows through the driest part of the United States. Water from the river is supplied to cities, such as Los Angeles and Las Vegas, and has turned the desert into farmland.

A boater sets off across the Salton Sea, one of several desert lakes filled by the Colorado River.

Left: A crowd of tourists gathers on an overlook in Grand Canyon National Park. The canyon is the most popular attraction on the river

The Colorado River was once the wildest river in what is now the United States. Today, it is the most tamed. This river of contrasts starts in the Rocky Mountains and winds through hot deserts before crossing into Mexico as it heads to the Gulf of California. The river once flowed to the Southwest's busiest seaports. Now, most of the river water is used before it reaches the ocean.

The modern Colorado River is the lifeline of the Southwest. Crossed by huge dams, it provides water and power for communities that otherwise could not exist in the desert.

Canyon, for example, the world's largest river canyon, is more than a mile deep (1.6 km) in some places.

Because the Colorado River flows through so much natural splendor, millions of people flock to the area to enjoy the amazing scenery and take part in water sports. They can sail on huge desert lakes that did not exist a hundred years ago or raft down mighty rapids in the hearts of beautiful canyons.

Below: Glen Canyon Dam holds back the Colorado River near Page, Arizona. The lake behind the dam holds over 8 trillion gallons (30 trillion liters) of water.

Red Rock River

Of the 1,450 miles (2,333 kilometers) that the Colorado flows, 1,380 miles (2,220 km) of it lies within the United States, making it the fifth-longest river in the nation. More than two-thirds of its length runs through deep canyons carved by the water into the red rocks of the area. The canyons are some of the most awesome natural sights in the United States. The Grand

From Source to Mouth

1

Flowing from the beautiful Rocky Mountains to the Gulf of California, the Colorado is an amazing river. Dams fill many of the river's canyons and create several artificial lakes.

Like all rivers, the Colorado starts life quietly. Its source is Shadow Mountain Lake high in the Rockies in the state of Colorado. The lake collects melted snow water from the tall peaks above. Emptying from the western end of the lake, the Colorado forms Lake Granby 5 miles (8 km) downstream before heading west and down through the mountains.

Into the Desert

At Grand Junction, Colorado, the Gunnison River empties into the Colorado. The Colorado River is already a huge river by the time it crosses into Utah.

Above Cataract Canyon in southeastern Utah, the Colorado is joined by the Green River, its largest tributary. The Green carries water from as far north as Wyoming and provides half of all the water in the Colorado River. Cataract Canyon has several fierce rapids, but the river soon broadens out into the calm Lake Powell, which stretches snakelike southwest for 186 miles (299 km). The San Juan River flows into this lake.

Lake Powell is created by the Glen Canyon Dam, which crosses the river just over the Arizona border. At the lake's southern end is the magnificent Rainbow Bridge—the largest rock arch in the world, which rises 309 feet (94 m) and spans 278 feet (85 m).

Right: *The fast-flowing Crystal River tumbles through the Rocky Mountains before meeting the Colorado River downstream of Lake Granby in Colorado.*

KEY FACTS	
Length:	1,450 miles (2,333 km)
Drainage basin:	246,000 square miles (637,140 sq km)
Source:	Shadow Mountain Lake, Colorado
Mouth:	Gulf of California
Natural features:	Grand Canyon, Marble Canyon, Glen Canyon
Economic uses:	Irrigation, hydroelectricity, water for cities, tourism
Major dams:	Glen Canyon Dam, Hoover Dam, Parker Dam
Major cities:	Grand Junction, Colorado; Yuma, Arizona; San Luis Río Colorado, Mexico

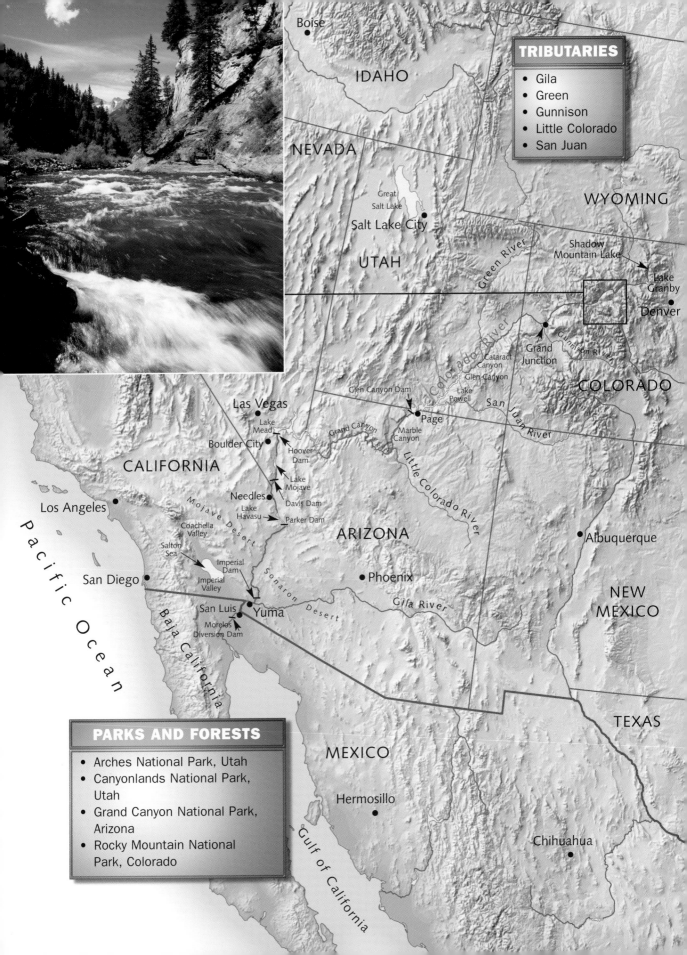

IDAHO

Boise

NEVADA

WYOMING

Great
Salt Lake

Salt Lake City

UTAH

Green River

Shadow
Mountain Lake

Lake
Granby

Denver

Grand
Junction

Gunnison River

COLORADO

Cataract
Canyon

Colorado River

Glen Canyon

Lake
Powell

San Juan River

Glen Canyon Dam

Page

Las Vegas

Lake
Mead

Grand Canyon

Marble
Canyon

Boulder City

Hoover
Dam

CALIFORNIA

Little Colorado River

Lake
Mojave

Needles

Davis Dam

Mojave Desert

Lake
Havasu

Parker Dam

ARIZONA

Los Angeles

Albuquerque

Coachella
Valley

Salton
Sea

NEW
MEXICO

Sonoran Desert

Imperial
Dam

Phoenix

San Diego

Imperial
Valley

Gila River

Pacific Ocean

San Luis

Yuma

Baja California

Morelos
Diversion Dam

TEXAS

MEXICO

Hermosillo

Chihuahua

Gulf of California

Above: *The Colorado makes a complete U-turn at Horseshoe Bend in Marble Canyon.*

Below: *This island in Lake Powell is named Gunsight Butte.*

Cutting through Rock

Below the Glen Canyon Dam, the Colorado is less turbulent than it once was because the dam cuts the flow of water by half. However, the river soon picks up strength again as it is fed by smaller rivers before it roars into the spectacular Marble Canyon. At the end of this canyon, the river is met by the Little Colorado River and enters the Grand Canyon, the world's largest and most famous canyon.

The 200-mile-long (322-km) Grand Canyon in Arizona was created over millions of years by the Colorado River. The water cut through rock, carving out a chasm a mile (1.6 km) deep. The rocks at the bottom of the Grand Canyon are more than two billion years old.

As the Grand Canyon ends, the enormous Lake Mead begins. The lake and the river beyond it form the border between the states of Arizona and Nevada. Lake Mead was created in 1935,

when the Hoover Dam was built. The lake now provides water for nearby Las Vegas, Nevada, and other cities farther west in California. Lake Mead is the largest artificial lake in the United States and took two years to fill after the dam was built.

So much water is taken from Lake Mead that the Colorado River's flow below the dam is just a trickle compared to what it once was. There is still enough water to fill other lakes, however. Lake Mojave and Lake Havasu are created by the Davis and Parker Dams.

Mexican River

As it flows toward Mexico, the Colorado River runs through two great deserts, the Mojave in California and

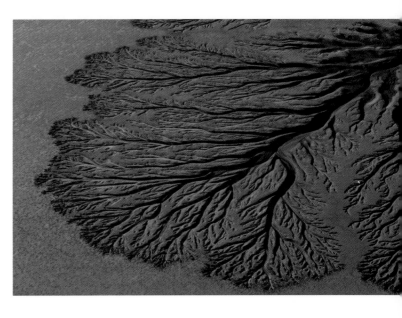

Above: *An aerial photo showing how the trickle of water that reaches the mouth of the river evaporates, producing these patterns in the river mud.*

the Sonoran in Arizona. The Sonoran is drained by the Gila River, which empties into the Colorado at Yuma, Arizona, near the Mexico border. The Colorado forms a 17-mile (27-km) border between the United States (Arizona) and Mexico (Baja California) before flowing entirely within Mexico. The river flows through Mexico for about 50 miles (80 km) before its path reaches the Gulf of California.

Just inside Mexico, the Morelos Diversion Dam feeds water into channels that supply irrigation for Mexico's crops. More often than not, this dam uses all of the river's remaining water. This means that unless there is a heavy rain and snow fall over Colorado, the Colorado River never reaches the ocean anymore.

2 The Life of the River

The Colorado flows from cold and wet mountains to hot and dry deserts. Because of this change in climate, the plants and animals that live near the river vary from its headwaters to its mouth.

In its northern reaches, the Colorado River twists through rocky canyons, past slopes cloaked with thick pine forests. Here, lynx and bobcats prowl in search of rabbits and ground-living birds, such as blue grouse.

In the branches above, other predators, such as hawks, owls, and eagles, keep watch as they hunt mice and other prey. On the ground, martens race after squirrels, and wolverines seek their own, larger prey. Except for porcupines, wolverines, which are giant relatives of weasels, will attack almost anything they encounter. Wolverines may even slide down steep slopes to attack mule deer that stray into

Below: *A pair of marmots beside a mountain lake near the head-waters of the Colorado River. Marmots are the largest type of squirrel.*

their range. Black bears, moose, and other large animals also roam through the riverside forests.

Land and Water
In more open areas, elk are common, as are coyotes and smaller creatures such as ground squirrels. Farther uphill, bighorn sheep live among the rocks and are preyed upon by mountain lions. When sheep are hard to find, the mountain lions make do with smaller prey, such as marmots and rabbits.

The fast-flowing river is home to a variety of fish. Strong swimmers, such as rainbow trout, live in the open water, while smaller, less powerful species shelter on the bottom. The bluehead sucker, for instance, hides among rocks, where it feeds on water plants. These fish sometimes fall prey to river otters—athletic swimmers that scour the Colorado River looking for food.

Warming Up
Farther downstream, the land gets hotter and drier. As the river leaves the mountains, it flows through gulches and canyons that at first seem empty of life.

Right: *A mountain lion crosses a waterfall in the mountains above the Colorado River in Utah.*

Many animals do live here, but few are active by day. The scorching heat means that most save their energy for feeding in the cool of the night. Jackrabbits lie still in whatever shade they can find, their long, silvery ears pressed against their backs to help reflect the Sun's heat. Smaller creatures dig burrows and keep cool underground. Kangaroo rats, for instance, spend the whole day lying in their dens. They even plug the entrance holes with dirt to keep the heat—and daytime hunters—out.

Hunted and Hunter

The kangaroo rat's worst enemy is the rattlesnake, but there are many others. Red-tailed hawks circle above by day, while at night, coyotes and kit foxes prowl with their ears open and their noses pressed to the ground. Coyotes and kit foxes also hunt other small animals, including antelope squirrels, wood rats, and chipmunks.

Large animals are rare in the deserts and dry canyons. One of the few to survive there is the bighorn sheep. Bighorns living in the very south of Utah and northern

THE RED RIVER

The Colorado (meaning "color red") River was named by the Spanish for its rich, red color. The color came from the red silt that the river carried downstream. Today, dams trap the silt that used to be carried by the river. Below the dams, the river water is now green (below).

Many of the river's fish were used to the red, muddy water. Since the dams cleared the water, many of these fish have died, and new species have moved in to take their place. Although it is not the river it once was, the Colorado continues to be a haven for wildlife.

GRAND CANYON RATTLESNAKE

One creature unique to the Colorado River is the Grand Canyon rattlesnake (right). As its name suggests, this rattler lives in the Grand Canyon and nowhere else. Its pinkish coloration and shy nature make it different from other rattlesnakes in the region. The Grand Canyon rattlesnake hunts by waiting patiently beside the tracks of rodents, waiting for its next meal to wander by. Although the snake has a rattle for warning, it hardly ever uses it. The snake is more likely to slither away than attack people and large animals that come too close. Only one person has ever been recorded as being bitten by a Grand Canyon rattlesnake —a climber who lived to tell the tale. The snake did not bite until the climber actually grabbed it by accident while clambering up the steep side of the canyon wall.

Arizona have thinner coats than those living up in the mountains. The sheep need to keep a sharp eye out for mountain lions and lynx, which will kill their lambs given a chance. As in the mountains, the river itself is home to otters and many fish. Beavers build dams across some of the creeks that flow into the river, and kingfishers and other birds live along its banks.

Below: *A bighorn ram (male sheep) rests on a Rocky Mountain ledge.*

3 A River in the Desert

Humans have lived beside the Colorado for thousands of years. Native people have long occupied its shores. The river was ruled by Spain and Mexico before it became primarily a U.S. river.

People have lived along the Colorado for ten thousand years. The first inhabitants of the area were the Clovis people. They used stone-tipped spears to hunt large animals, such as elephant-like mammoths, which are now extinct. The first Clovis people were nomadic and survived by following the animals they hunted.

Change of Life

About eight thousand years ago, however, everything changed as the large animals died out. With no herds left to follow, the people altered the way they lived. They turned to hunting smaller animals and searched for fruits and roots. They also began to settle down, living mostly in one place. These people created objects and art that can still be seen today, including impressive rock paintings in what is now called the Great Gallery in Canyonlands National Park.

About two thousand years ago, two new groups of Native people arrived in the Colorado River region: the Hohokam and Anasazi. These people lived in present-day Arizona. The Hohokam were expert farmers, growing corn,

Below: *Two Hualapai boys stand on the rim of the Grand Canyon. The Hualapai people have lived by the Colorado River for more than a thousand years.*

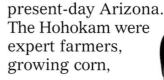

Above: *An Arizona Navajo family grows corn in 1889. Their shelter is called a hogan.*

beans, and squashes. They used elaborate irrigation systems that were fed by creeks that ran into the river. About seven hundred years ago, these people vanished, leaving their homes behind. No one knows why, but perhaps the climate changed and less water was available.

At first, the Anasazi lived as nomads in the region near the Grand Canyon, hunting and gathering plants. They later began to farm and build villages. The Anasazi were probably the ancestors of the Southwest's modern Pueblo people.

New People
About three hundred years ago, the Navajo people moved south and settled among the Pueblo peoples.

MOJAVE FARMERS

The Colorado River's southern reaches were farmed by a Native group called the Mojave. The Mojave traveled along the Colorado using rafts made of reeds, trading their crops of pumpkins, melons, corn, and squashes. Mojave men (below) often had to defend their fertile land from neighboring groups. The name Mojave means "three mountains" and comes from the three peaks that loom over the river near the modern California town of Needles.

During much of this time, the upper section of the river was home to the Ute people. The Ute rarely stayed in one place and moved through the hills in search of large animals. Utah was named for the Ute people when it became a state in 1896.

Today, there are several Native reservations along the Colorado, including the Navajo Nation, which borders the southern shores of Lake Powell and is about the size of Rhode Island.

Spanish Visitors

The first Europeans to see the Colorado were Spanish. In 1540, an expedition set off from Mexico (then ruled by Spain) in search of Cibola—a legendary land that was thought to have cities made from gold.

The explorers did not find any golden cities, but they did see the Colorado River. Before long, explorers had reached the Grand Canyon. Some explorers crossed the river farther south into what is now California.

Mexican Rule

In 1598, the Spanish claimed a territory they named New Mexico. Much bigger than the modern state, their New Mexico stretched from the Colorado River in the west to western parts of Texas. Although ruled by Spain, most of the people who lived there were Native to the area. Spain's rule there lasted for more than two centuries.

In 1821, Mexico gained independence from Spain and with it the control of New Mexico and much of

Below: *John Wesley Powell (fifth from right) on his second journey down the Colorado River in 1871.*

PEOPLE OF BLUE-GREEN WATER

Deep below the Grand Canyon's southern rim, Havasu Canyon is home to the Havasupai people. Their name means "people of blue-green water" after the water of Havasu Creek, which tumbles through their land. This small creek collects most of the rainwater that falls south of the Grand Canyon and turns the Havasupai's little canyon into a fertile green oasis. The creek flows strongly all year, falling over beautiful waterfalls as it makes its way to the Colorado River. No road reaches the reservation's village. Food and supplies are carried in by mules. Many visitors to the reservation travel in and out of the canyon by helicopter.

the Colorado River. Even though the river was now part of Mexican territory, little else changed. The river itself continued to flow as it always had, uninterrupted from the Rocky Mountains all the way to the Gulf of California.

Mexico's control of the Colorado River lasted for just twenty-six years. In 1847, U.S. soldiers captured Mexico City and forced the country's leader to sign a treaty that gave the United States ownership of a huge amount of Mexican land. The new U.S. territory covered what is now the states of California, Nevada, Arizona, Utah, and parts of present-day New Mexico, Texas, Colorado, and Wyoming. In return, Mexico was given eighteen million dollars.

From then on, the Colorado River flowed almost entirely through U.S. territory. To everyone except its Native residents, however, the river remained a bit of a mystery. No one knew the length of the river or its source, and

Above: *Havasu Falls in the Havasupai Indian Reservation is one of three waterfalls along Havasu Creek. Havasu Creek flows to the Colorado River at the southern rim of the Grand Canyon.*

only a few non-Native people had ever seen its amazing natural features.

Down the River

The first known non-Native person to travel down the Colorado was a Civil War veteran named John Wesley Powell. A close friend of U.S. president Ulysses Grant, he led an expedition down the river in 1869.

Powell's journey began on the Green River in Wyoming. Together with his brother Walter and eight unpaid volunteers, Powell set off with four flat-bottomed boats. One of the boats was smashed apart on rocks before they reached the Colorado River. Three made it through to Cataract Canyon, where the rapids were so powerful that the explorers were forced to carry the boats around them. Eventually, the explorers made it through the Grand Canyon.

At the end of the Grand Canyon, where the Virgin River flowed into the Colorado (a section that is now under Lake Mead), John Wesley Powell left the river. Two expedition members continued all the way to the Gulf of California. John Wesley Powell repeated his historic journey two years later, and on this trip, he took his time. He recorded his journey in great detail, and, when he returned, Powell wrote a book about the river.

Empty Land

Without the water of the Colorado River, the quality of life enjoyed today by most of the Southwest's

Above: *A steamboat and coal barge on the Colorado River near a Nevada gold mine in 1890.*

citizens would not exist. Most of the Southwest was a wilderness 150 years ago. The Colorado River had not been mapped properly, and few settlers came to the area.

Soon, however, the river was used as a route from the Pacific Ocean into southern California and Arizona. Between 1850 and 1880, the stretch from the Gulf of California to the port of Yuma was thick with ships carrying provisions. When gold was discovered near where the Colorado and Gila Rivers meet, many miners rushed into the area.

Water Law

In the early twentieth century, the population of southern California grew rapidly, and people needed water. Under the law at the time, the first people to use water from the river had the right to do so forever. People arriving later could only use the water left over. This law seemed fair because there was enough water in the river for everyone. Later, however, the huge demand for water meant that the law had to be changed.

ACCIDENTAL SEA

Soon after the Colorado River became U.S. property, settlers began using the Colorado's water to irrigate desert farms. In 1905, the river burst through poorly built irrigation channels and flooded a low-lying area of California known as the Salton Basin. Two years later, the water flow was finally stopped, but by then, the whole basin was more than 30 feet (9 meters) underwater (below). The Salton Basin has never emptied. Today it is known as the Salton Sea and is the largest lake in California.

4 Taming the Wild River

From California to Utah, nearly every aspect of life in the Southwest depends on the Colorado River. The river waters the dry land and provides power and drinking water to desert cities.

The Colorado has always been a major focus for life in the dry Southwest. In the last century, however, its waters transformed the land, turning dry scrub and desert into productive fields. Before World War I (1914–1918), farming in the area was small scale and there was plenty of irrigation water for every farmer.

Above: *A canal carries Colorado River water across the desert in California.*

Sharing Water

By the 1920s, governments of states along the Colorado River were getting worried that there soon might not be enough water for the needs of their citizens.

The number of people living in California was growing fast. Under the law as it stood, Californians had the rights to use most of the river's water. If California owned the water, other states would not be able to use any for themselves. Something had to be done.

In 1922, California agreed to share the river with six other states. Half of the water from the Colorado belongs to the Upper Basin states (Wyoming, Colorado, Utah, and New Mexico), and the other half belongs to the Lower Basin states (California, Arizona, and Nevada). In addition, the United States must leave a supply of water in the river for Mexico. This is generally not enough water to reach the ocean, however.

California has the rights to most of the water, followed by Colorado and Arizona. Most of the water is used by farmers or sent to Los Angeles and other cities. However, growing states are now demanding a larger share of water.

Below: *Tourists ride through the Grand Canyon on mules. Colorado River tourism is an important industry.*

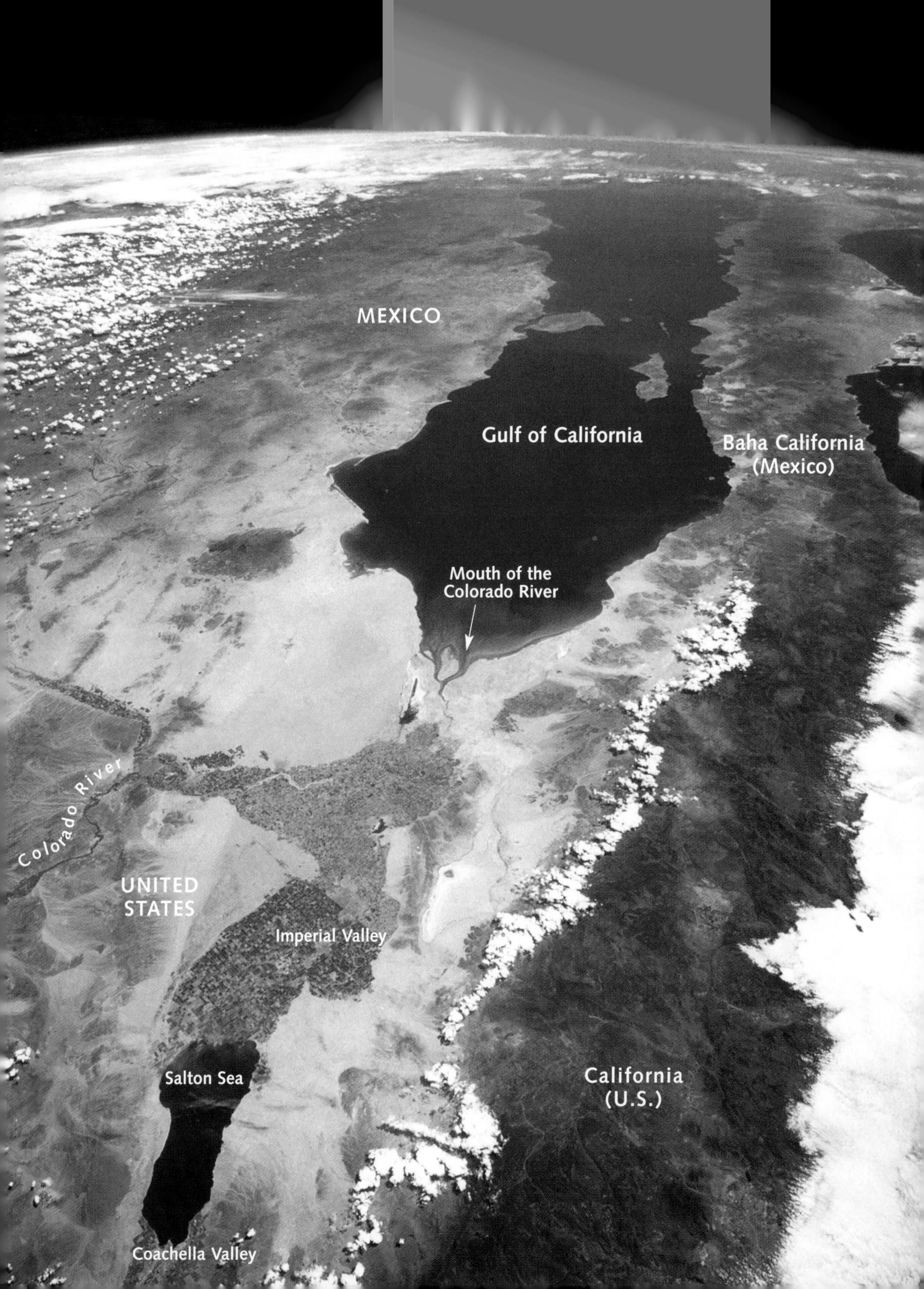

MEXICO

Gulf of California

Baha California
(Mexico)

Mouth of the
Colorado River

Colorado River

UNITED
STATES

Imperial Valley

Salton Sea

California
(U.S.)

Coachella Valley

HOOVER DAM

When it was built in the 1930s, Hoover Dam was heavier and taller than any other dam in the world. Plans for the dam were supported by President Herbert Hoover, who was an engineer. Hoover knew that the dam would prevent floods and store water to irrigate farmland and supply desert cities. The government planned to pay for the dam by selling the electricity it made.

Construction of the dam (intake towers, right) started in 1931 and took nearly five years. It was a huge operation. Before work began, a new town—Boulder City, Nevada—was built to house the workers. Trapeze artists were employed to hang inside the canyon and clear loose rocks from the walls. Two temporary dams were built to divert the Colorado River. The main dam was put together from cubes of concrete. Enough concrete was used to pave a highway from San Francisco to New York City.

Left: *An image taken by a satellite (looking south) shows how Colorado River water has turned parts of Southern California's deserts green.*

Watering the Desert

One hundred years ago, California's Imperial Valley and Coachella Valley were parched wastelands. Today, they make up one of the most productive farming areas in the country.

The change is thanks to Colorado River water, which is diverted into the valleys by two long canals. The 80-mile-long (129-km) All-American Canal carries water to the Imperial Valley from a lake behind Imperial Dam, a few miles upstream from Yuma, Arizona. The 123-mile-long (198-km) Coachella Canal branches off the All-American Canal taking water northwest around the Salton Sea.

Farms in the two valleys grow cotton, grapes, and oranges even in the winter, when many farms elsewhere in the country are unable to grow crops.

Supplying Cities

For most of its history, the Colorado River was untamed, and the people who lived alongside it lived with its natural cycles. The river flooded repeatedly, washing away homes and farms and making it hard to develop the area. Damming the river has changed that.

LAS VEGAS—THE DESERT CITY

Las Vegas owes its life to the Colorado River. Without the river, the city could not exist. Las Vegas was founded in 1905. Its population then survived on water from a group of natural springs. Today, almost every drop of water in the city comes from Lake Mead on the river. Las Vegas and its suburbs are home to 1.5 million people, and many thousands visit the city's casinos and attractions every day. It is one of the fastest growing cities in the country.

Left: *The bright lights of the Las Vegas Strip are illuminated by electricity generated by Hoover Dam.*

The first dam across the Colorado River was the Hoover Dam, completed in 1935. It was built partly to produce electricity and partly to control flooding. A year before Hoover Dam was finished, work began on Parker Dam, 155 miles (249 km) downstream.

Parker Dam was built for a different purpose. Its job was to create a reservoir of water—Lake Havasu—to supply water to the growing cities in Southern California. Parker Dam was completed in 1938, and the lake behind it slowly filled. In 1941, water finally began to flow into another giant canal, the Colorado River Aqueduct, which ran all the way to the Pacific coast. Today, the Colorado River Aqueduct and the San Diego Aqueduct, which branches off of it, provide 1 billion gallons (3.8 billion liters) of water every day to Los Angeles and other cities in Southern California.

Between 1973 and 1992, a new system was linked to Lake Havasu, this time on its eastern shore. Called the Central Arizona Project, it consists of a series of pumps and canals that take water to places all over central and southern Arizona.

Below: *The tops of the Hoover Dam's four intake towers stick out from the surface of Lake Mead. Lake water flows into the towers and drives generators inside the dam.*

northern border. In 1963, it was built to generate electricity, and it holds back the huge Lake Powell, named after explorer John Wesley Powell. The other three dams—Imperial Dam, Laguna Dam, and Morelos Diversion Dam—were built as part of irrigation projects.

River Tourism

The Colorado River is a haven for pleasure-seekers. The Grand Canyon is the United States' number one tourist attraction. It receives five million visitors a year. Some people come for just a few hours to see the spectacular scenery; others stay longer. There is plenty to keep people busy in Grand Canyon National Park. One of the most popular activities is taking a mule ride to the canyon floor, a mile (1.6 km) below.

The pumps are needed because most of Arizona is up higher than Lake Havasu. In fact, by the time it gets to some of its destinations, the water has been lifted nearly 2,900 feet (884 m).

Controlling Flow

The third dam to be built across the Colorado was the Davis Dam, about 10 miles (16 km) north of the point where Arizona, California, and Nevada meet. Finished in 1953, its job was to regulate releases of water from the much bigger Hoover Dam upstream and help with flood control.

There are four other dams on the Colorado River. The largest of those is Glen Canyon Dam on Arizona's

Above: *Workers prepare a huge pipe to carry river water to Phoenix, Arizona.*

Below: *Rafters shoot the rapids at Lava Falls deep in the Grand Canyon.*

Another is rafting down the river inside the canyon. Many people like to take a smooth-water journey, but some go whitewater rafting, shooting the rapids in giant inflatable boats.

A few of the visitors to the Grand Canyon go hiking and camp out under the stars, but most prefer to stay high on the canyon rim enjoying the view. Horseback riding and climbing are popular. Tourists can take helicopter or airplane rides over the canyon, too.

Less Traveled

Of course, the Grand Canyon is not the only attraction along the Colorado River, and many other places get plenty of visitors as well. Farther upstream in Utah is Lake Powell, with its incredible Rainbow Bridge and Canyonlands National Park, which includes The Maze—an extremely remote rugged desert. In Colorado, the beautiful Rocky Mountains also offer many opportunities for recreation and sightseeing.

BRINGING WATER THROUGH THE MOUNTAINS

At the end of the nineteenth century, northeastern Colorado was developing fast. The fertile South Platte River Valley was rapidly being turned into farmland, and water was needed to irrigate crops. At first, water from the South Platte River was used, but soon this was not enough, and people started looking for a new source of water. In 1889, an answer was found. The South Platte ran down the eastern side of the Rocky Mountains, but on the western slopes was a mightier river—the Colorado. All that was needed was to take water from the Colorado and somehow get it across the mountains. After many years of planning, work began on a tunnel through the mountains in 1938. Called the Adams Tunnel, it links the Colorado to the Big Thompson River— a tributary of the South Platte. When the tunnel was finished in 1947, the water it carried supplied farms and the city of Denver, Colorado (below), which grew into a major metropolitan area.

5 Places to Visit

About ten million people use the Colorado River for recreation every year. They hike, camp, climb, swim, sail, fish, visit the dams, or just enjoy the spectacular scenery and historic sites.

❸

❶ Rocky Mountain National Park, Colorado
The headwaters of the Colorado begin in this rugged park. The park includes the mighty Longs Peak, which is more than 14,000 feet (4,267 m) high.

❷ Arches National Park, Utah
Huge underground forces have bent blocks of red sandstone into spires and arches, which have since been eroded into formations by wind and rain.

❸ Rainbow Bridge, Lake Powell, Utah
Rainbow Bridge (left) is a natural rock arch on the shore of Lake Powell, close to the Glen Canyon Dam. The lake is popular with fishers and boaters.

④ Bryce Canyon National Park, Utah
The freakish landscape of Bryce Canyon makes it a unique place to visit. The amazing canyon (above) is filled with red and yellow pillars of stone called hoodoos.

⑤ Grand Canyon, Arizona
The Grand Canyon is the most popular tourist attraction on the Colorado River. The tourist village on South Rim is the best place to start exploring the canyon.

⑥ Las Vegas, Nevada
Millions of U.S. and foreign tourists visit the city of Las Vegas to gamble in its casinos, catch flashy shows by international entertainers, or enjoy the famous sights and sounds of the Strip.

⑧ Salton Sea, California
Created by floodwaters from the Colorado, this lake is a popular visitor attraction in the middle of the Mojave Desert.

⑨ Yuma, Arizona
One of the Southwest's oldest cities, Yuma was the major crossing point of the Colorado River during California's Gold Rush and has several historic sites nearby.

⑩ Baja California, Mexico
The Colorado River used to pour into the Gulf of California between the mainland of Mexico and the Baja Peninsula. Today, the Colorado is little more than a trickle at its mouth. However, the unique wildlife of the area, including unusual desert trees and the Cortez harbor porpoise, make it an interesting place to visit.

7 London Bridge, Lake Havasu, Arizona

The most famous bridge on the Colorado River is London Bridge. Transported from London, England, the bridge joins an island in Lake Havasu to its eastern shore. The bridge (right) was bought in 1968 by Robert P. McCullock, the founder of Lake Havasu City. He paid ten million dollars for it, but rumors abound that he bought the wrong bridge. Some say he meant to buy Tower Bridge, a more famous bridge in London. Others suggest he thought he was getting the thirteenth-century version of London Bridge. The bridge he got is about 170 years old and was replaced by a new London Bridge in 1967 because the old bridge was sinking in mud and cracking up.

How Rivers Form

Rivers have many features that are constantly changing in shape. The illustration below shows how these features are created.

Rivers flow from mountains to oceans, receiving water from rain, melting snow, and underground springs. Rivers collect their water from an area called the river basin. High mountain ridges form the divides between river basins.

Tributaries join the main river at places called confluences. Rivers flow down steep mountain slopes quickly but slow as they near the ocean and gather more water. Slow rivers have many meanders (wide turns) and often change course.

Near the mouth, levees (piles of mud) build up on the banks. The levees stop water from draining into the river, creating areas of swamp.

❶ Glacier: An ice mass that melts into river water.

❷ Lake: The source of many rivers; may be fed by springs or precipitation.

❸ Rapids: Shallow water that flows quickly.

❹ Waterfall: Formed when a river wears away softer rock, making a step in the riverbed.

❺ Canyon: Formed when a river cuts a channel through rock.

❻ Floodplain: A place where rivers often flood flat areas, depositing mud.

❼ Oxbow lake: River bend cut off when a river changes course, leaving water behind.

❽ Estuary: River mouth where river and ocean water mix together.

❾ Delta: Triangular river mouth created when mud islands form, splitting the flow into several channels called distributaries.

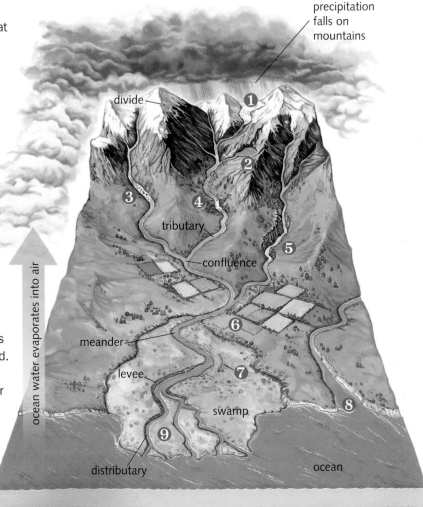

precipitation falls on mountains

divide

tributary

confluence

ocean water evaporates into air

meander

levee

swamp

distributary

ocean

Glossary

artificial Made by people.

basin The area drained by a river and its tributaries.

chasm A deep opening in the ground.

confluence The place where rivers meet.

dam A constructed barrier across a river that controls the flow of water.

generator A machine that turns mechanical energy into electricity.

gulch A deep space or opening, like a ravine.

gulf A part of an ocean that extends into land.

headwaters The source of a river, where water is collected from the surrounding land.

industry Producing things or providing services in order to earn money.

irrigation Watering crops with water from a river, lake, or other source.

oasis A fertile area surrounded by desert.

predator An animal that gets its food by hunting or ambushing other animals.

prey An animal hunted for food.

reservation An area of land set aside for a particular purpose. Many Natives live on reservations created by the government.

rodent An animal, such as a rat or mouse, with front teeth used for gnawing.

silt Very fine particles of sand or clay that are carried along on river currents. When the current slows, the silt settles to the bottom of the river.

source The place where a river begins.

tributary A river that flows into a larger river at a confluence.

valley A hollow channel cut by a river, usually between ranges of hills or mountains.

For Further Information

Books

Inskip, Eleanor. *The Colorado River through Glen Canyon: Before Lake Powell.* Inskip Ink, 1995.

Ladd, Gary. *Lake Powell.* Companion Press, 1994.

Powell, John W. *Exploration of the Colorado River and Its Canyons.* Dover Publications, 1961.

Rawlins, Carol B. *The Colorado River.* Franklin Watts, 1999.

Web Sites

Canyonlands Photo Gallery
www.nps.gov/cany/gallery

Friends of Lake Powell
www.lakepowell.org

Grand Canyon National Park
www.nps.gov/grca/grandcanyon

Hoover Dam
www.hooverdam.usbr.gov

Salton Sea
www.saltonsea.ca.gov

Index

DATE DUE

FOLLETT